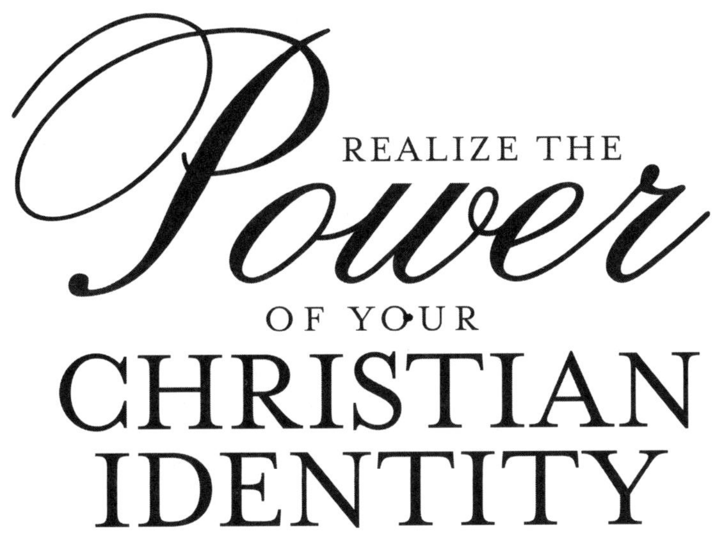
REALIZE THE
Power
OF YOUR
CHRISTIAN
IDENTITY

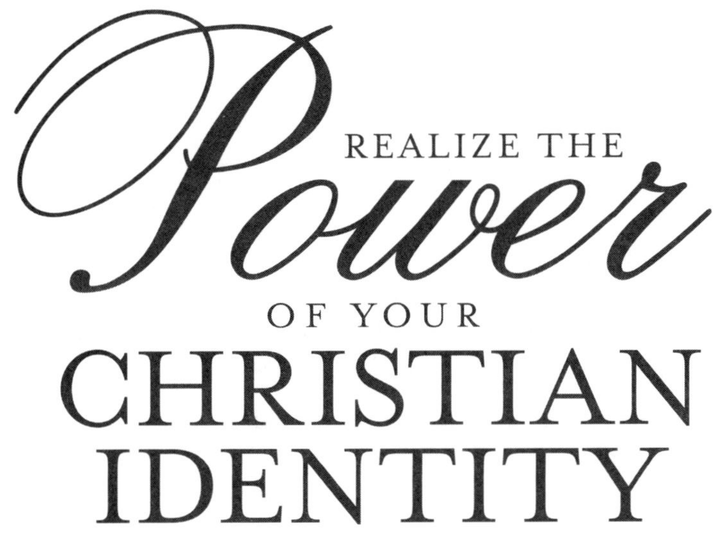

REALIZE THE

Power

OF YOUR

CHRISTIAN IDENTITY

Julie Ngwabi

CREATION **HOUSE**

REALIZE THE POWER OF YOUR CHRISTIAN IDENTITY
By Julie Ngwabi
Published by Creation House
A Charisma Media Company
600 Rinehart Road
Lake Mary, Florida 32746
www.charismamedia.com

Unless otherwise noted, all Scripture quotations are from the Holy Bible, New International Version. Copyright © 1973, 1978, 1984, 2010, 2011, International Bible Society. Used by permission.

Scripture quotations marked KJV are from the King James Version of the Bible.

Design Director: Bill Johnson
Cover design by Nathan Morgan

Visit the author's website: www.christianidentity.com.au

Library of Congress Cataloging-in-Publication Data:
2012955804
International Standard Book Number: 978-1-62136-340-8
E-book International Standard Book Number:
978-1-62136-341-5

First edition

13 14 15 16 17 — 987654321
Printed in Canada

DEDICATION

THIS BOOK IS dedicated to my loving husband, Bornwell, for his support and encouragement in pursuing the will of God in my life. Also to Arnold, my darling son with a beautiful, kind, gentle spirit. I thank my mother, Jane, for persevering and holding onto her faith during the difficult times. To my dearest sisters, Samkeliso and Saida, and my brothers, Charles and Mgcini; you will always be part of my life.

ACKNOWLEDGMENTS

I THANK THE HOLY Spirit for His guidance throughout the process, without which this book would not have been.

I thank God for Pastor Meredith Baker of Freedom City Church in Sydney; I greatly appreciate your support, prayer, and encouragement, amazing inspiring woman of God.

I will always deeply appreciate the staff at Creation House/Charisma Media, Ann Stoner, Allen Quain, Robert Caggiano, Stephanie Arena, and Brenda Davis. I say, "God bless you."

TABLE OF CONTENTS

Foreword xiii

Introduction 1

1 The Different Identities and Titles of Life 5

2 Salvation: The Source of a Believer's Identity 11

3 We Have Been Saved by Grace 21

4 Only Jesus Can Make Us Whole. 27

5 God's Spirit Guides Us to Live Out Our
   True Identities 31

6 Who We Are Never Lets Go 37

7 Treasure Your Identity 47

8 God Never Gives Up on Us 59

9 God Wants Us to Let Go of the "Good" Past
   As Well 65

10 We Have Been Predestined by God 69

11 We Are Christ's Ambassadors. 77

12 We Are Living Epistles for Christ. 85

13 We Are Called to Imitate Christ. 93

14 The Lord Will Fight Our Battles. 99

About the Author 105

Contact the Author 107

FOREWORD

Have you been guilty of judging by first appearances or first impressions? We can be so easily intimidated by the person who seems to have it "all together"—they dress well, speak confidently, and appear so self-assured.

How many people wear a mask, put on a good front, strive and struggle to be accepted, spend endless dollars to do what it takes to gain approval, and yet inside remain empty, confused, and even lonely, longing to discover their identity. Just where do I fit? Who am I really? Does anyone care?

Julie's book magnificently addresses all the above. I have savored every page and have a fresh appreciation of my life and my value, my purpose and, above all, my God. I am precious, important to God, and so are you!

There are many Christians who don't truly understand their identity in Christ and how it can empower their lives. It is so liberating to unmask the deceptions we once settled for.

Society globally has radically changed with the increase of cross-pollination of cultures, creating a diversity of lifestyles and traditions. We also have a greater proportion of family domestic complications—and these two lifestyle challenges alone can leave individuals desperately seeking a sense of belonging or searching out their roots in a bid to discover their identity that will confirm they are wanted and loved, and which affirms they do have a purpose on this planet.

I first met Julie when she and her husband attended an evening service in our church. My first impression was that this lady has dignity, presents beautifully, has a graceful, humble confidence, and loves to worship God. I had no idea of her painful childhood in Zimbabwe, the struggles and humiliation she experienced which led to her newfound identity as a believer, aged just fifteen. She then began to navigate her way to victory as she applied the Word of truth. Julie testifies we can all be overcomers and discover as she did that God has a good plan for our lives.

Later when reading her book, it was evident Julie was writing from a personal, life changing experience. It is very engaging. She has a magnificent ability to weave the Word of God into her dialogue so that it strengthens her compelling explanation of every facet of our identity as a child of God, and leaves no doubt that Jesus conquered all life's challenges so we can live life to the full.

I was repeatedly refreshed to read about various personalities in the Bible whose lives Julie uses to colorfully enhance her explanations of God's faithfulness and to encourage us that He is always in control, loves us unconditionally, and is a loving Father.

This book will take you on a journey of discovering your new life and new identity as a born-again believer. You won't want to put it down it's so easy to read and digest. Julie has been able to unfold so beautifully a truth that will set you free to be *the you* God planned for you to be. Read it, love it, and live it.

—Pastor Meredith Baker
Freedom City Church, Sydney, Australia

INTRODUCTION

The world gives us different identities from the moment we are born, through life, and up until the very end when we die. From these identities we assume various roles and responsibilities; and these may bring us joy, pride, and a sense of belonging, yet on the other hand stress, pain, and even sadness. Therefore, the number of identities we acquire through the natural process of life can either complement each other or cause strife or conflict in our lives, unless there is a solid foundation from which we can be able to maintain normalcy and stability, apart from which we risk feeling like we are being pulled from different directions. Christians are no exception.

From the instant we are born, before we may even have a name, the midwife or whoever is doing the delivery shouts, "It's a boy!" Or, "It's a girl!" Right there and then, when we first make our contact with the world, already we are given a title or identity. However, when we get saved or born again, something magnificent happens to us.

There is a great transformation which takes place inside which revolutionizes and changes us forever. We do not necessarily feel it with our senses because it happens in the spiritual realm. "Why in the spirit and not in my flesh or soul?" you ask. Because God is a Spirit, He cannot dwell anywhere else but in your spirit. According to John 4:24, "God is spirit, and his worshipers must worship in spirit and in truth."

We are human beings even as Christians; we get born naturally and go through the changes of life, we live on this earth just like everybody else, yet really we are spiritual beings who live in physical bodies and have souls. The Spirit of God comes to reside in your spirit upon salvation, hence the Bible says we become God's temples (1 Cor. 6:19).

We become one with God when His Spirit is joined to our spirits, and this is what being born again is all about. This miraculous birth and transformation which takes place spiritually is the foundation and rock by which we can live victorious, successful, peaceful, and meaningful lives as we begin to realize who we really are as the children of God. We begin to fully appreciate our salvation which came as a result of Jesus' death and resurrection, and we embark on seeing ourselves from God's perspective as we now belong to Him. If we identify ourselves as the children of the almighty living God who loves us beyond human comprehension, we can trust Him that He only wants the best for us. And if we totally submit to Him, we can live purposeful and satisfying lives as He begins to transform us into Christ's likeness.

In the midst of a chaotic and ever changing world, as children of God we can enjoy peace and stability when we know that we have victory and life from the inside that can make it possible for us to withstand whatever the world may throw at us. In truth it does not matter what our circumstances are like or what roles or responsibilities we have to fulfill, everything else falls into its perspective place, just like a piece of puzzle; you have to get that one big piece right then the rest will be easier. As a Christian that is knowing that first and foremost you are a child of God.

Chapter 1

THE DIFFERENT IDENTITIES
AND TITLES OF LIFE

WHEN WE ARE born, we are given names by family members. A name can be chosen for various reasons. It could be after a beloved friend or relative, dead or alive, and sometimes with the hope that the child may have some of the desirable characteristics of that dear person. In the case of a deceased relative, it may be hoped that their memory will continue.

Some people choose names because they like how they resonate whether or not their meaning is known. Unfortunately, maybe just like me, you know of people whose names have nothing inspiring or positive at all about them whatsoever. Names like Doubt, War, Pain, and the like. Although there is usually a story or meaning behind them, personally I have never understood why a new life should be burdened with such negativity and heaviness in a name.

As we go through life, we obtain titles or identities along the way. We enroll in school and become students. We have different titles or identities to our siblings—we become brothers and sisters, and nephews and nieces to other family members. We are identified differently to the rest of the community and to our neighbors and friends. And these bring us some sense of belonging, joy, and security as well as certain responsibilities.

We may eventually go to college and become graduates or dropouts, if for some reasons we do not finish college. As will be discussed later, there are some identities in life we have power, choice, and control over, whereas others are just inevitable. Later we may be employed and be known as employees and workers. We get married and have our own children and before you know it, we are parents ourselves. As we are all aware, this is not necessarily a concrete sequence of events for everybody; but it illustrates that as we get older in life, our identities, roles, and responsibilities change whether we are born again or not. And, if we do not have a stable foundation from which these changes occur, we might find ourselves feeling lost, overwhelmed, and even fragmented. Having mentioned that; God does want us to excel in our studies, to marry the right partners, and have kids as predestined by Him and according to the plans and purposes for our individual lives.

On the other hand and from our perspective, in life we may cope with undesirable or unforeseen circumstances. My father died when I was eleven years old. I did not choose to be an orphan at that age, and neither did my mother anticipate being a widow at thirty-five. Situations do happen in life that we have no control of; suddenly we are known and referred to differently by no choice of ours. Unexpectedly, life is not as we had known or anticipated it to be.

But praise be to God our Father because He is always in ultimate control of our lives despite the circumstances and He will take care of us. Victory is assured if we submit to Him and trust Him that everything will turn out right. No loving father allows his children to go where they will be harmed. It seems as though as Christians, when we face challenges, God wants the world to watch and see how things will work out for us simply because we are Christians. The Bible says, "But thanks be to God, who always leads us in triumphal procession in Christ and through us spreads everywhere the fragrance of the knowledge of him" (2 Cor. 2:14).

IDENTITIES MAY COMPLEMENT OR CONFLICT EACH OTHER

Whether you are a working parent or a student, there are times when you have to wear different hats to suit the different occasions. It may appear like there is barely time to remove one and put on another as required. A student's responsibility may overflow from the school-yard into the family home in the form of homework or after school activities like sports. I remember coming home from school, doing homework, and then looking after my young brothers and sisters. As the big sister and oldest child, I had the responsibility of helping our mother with house chores and taking care of my siblings. I was the big sister and daughter, and as such I assumed a significant portion of responsibility around the house; but at the same time I still had to make time to study and do my homework.

My mother was a firm believer in the importance of getting an education. From an early age I found myself juggling different roles and tasks as was expected from my position in the family. As a young girl I still needed to go out and be with my friends, and I would struggle to find the time to be with them. Thankfully they understood my situation and my close friends would come and help me around the house so that I could go out with them.

With the prevailing economic climate, most people have to work. They juggle that with their roles as parents, spouses, and church activities and responsibilities. There is so much to do and so many demands on us, at times we feel like we are drowning or spiraling out of control. This is all because of the different identities we have, each with its own demands, but all in one individual.

Most of the time we labor to strike a balance or harmony, given the various expectations. Sometimes these roles may even conflict with each other. For example, let's just say you are a father trying to be a good role model to your children by telling them smoking and alcohol are bad for them and you happen to work in the advertising industry. Suddenly you are required to promote a brand of cigarettes or alcohol openly. Your role as an employee may conflict with your role as a parent, and your children will ask you where you stand. Thankfully, as Christians and children of God, we can be guided by what the Word of God says about such situations.

However, as Christians there is hope for us. God knows that in this life we will have different roles and responsibilities to fulfill, and as such He has made provision for His children to effectively perform them without losing sense of self and feeling overwhelmed. For challenging times that we may experience, He is right there with us to bring us peace and comfort.

God Promises a Light Load

This juggling act can leave us weary and worn out. But glory be to God because there is a rest that is found in Christ. Jesus said:

> Come to me, all you who are weary and burdened, and I will give you rest. Take my yoke upon you and learn from me, for I am gentle and humble in heart, and you will find rest for your souls. For my yoke is easy and my burden is light.
>
> —Matthew 11:28–30

This is not the kind of rest that comes from spending time in a spa or massage parlor; neither is it a rest for the soul you find from a therapist's couch. It's a rest that comes from knowing Jesus and surrendering our demanding and heavy loads unto Him. We do not have to labor or strive for it; we simply call upon Him and enter into it. When we have this rest we are then able to effectively do what we need to do and fulfill our other roles from the strength only He can give us as the children of God. Paul says in Philippians 4:13, "I can do everything through him who gives me strength."

Chapter 2

SALVATION: THE SOURCE OF A BELIEVER'S IDENTITY

WHEN GOD CREATED Adam and Eve, He gave them dominion over all other creation. Man has always been special to God and is set apart in that he was made in God's own image.

> Then God said, "Let us make man in our image, in our likeness, and let them rule over the fish of the sea and the birds of the air, over the livestock, over all the earth, and over all the creatures that move along the ground." So God created man over his own image, in the image of God he created him; male and female he created them. God blessed them and said to them, "Be fruitful and increase in number; fill the earth and subdue it. Rule over the fish of the sea and the birds that of the air and over every living creature that moves on the ground."
> —GENESIS 1:26–28

God created the light, stars, and vegetation and separated water from the land; and it was all good. Though all the other magnificent creation was made by God

Himself and was beautiful, it was not made in His image. But man was made in His own image and likeness!

Furthermore, man was given dominion over all the other creation and the responsibility to take care of it. Moreover God blessed them (v. 28). We don't hear that He did the same to the other creatures. Not only are we made from His image but the very first breath man ever took came from God Himself!

> The Lord God formed the man from the dust of the ground and breathed into his nostrils the breath of life, and the man became a living being.
> —Genesis 2:7

We were made unique and special because God from the very beginning intended to have a close relationship with us; we were always more than just another of His many creations, just like you are not just one of the Christians but are a unique and distinctive individual child of God.

Sin Separated Us from God, but Jesus Reconciled Us to Him

When the first man was deceived by the serpent, sin entered into the world and separated man from God. In the garden when God came looking for Adam and Eve for their usual fellowship, they hid from Him because suddenly they felt ashamed and naked (Gen. 3:8). Something had changed and tainted their relationship; they had sinned against God and therefore no longer felt confident and comfortable in His presence. If God has a plan for your life, guess what? The devil has got one for you too! He wants to separate you from God's presence; and he knows that you are lost, powerless, and vulnerable without God.

Despite Adam's sin, which we all inherited from him, God has never stopped loving us. Adam might have brought sin and subsequent death to mankind, but God already had a plan to redeem and make us righteous through Jesus Christ.

> For just as through the disobedience of the one man the many were made sinners, so also through the obedience of the one man the many will be made righteous.
>
> —ROMANS 5:19

When we are born again we are made right again with God; that is why the Bible says we become His righteousness. Our sin was atoned for once and for all through the shedding of the blood of Jesus Christ. He was blameless, holy, and righteous; therefore, He was the only one who could reconcile and restore our fellowship and relationship with the almighty God.

> God made him who had no sin to be sin for us, so that in him we might become the righteousness of God.
>
> —2 CORINTHIANS 5:21

Just as God did not renounce His love and longing for us then, He will never give up on us today whether we are born again or not. Every day with Him is a chance for a new beginning. In the story of the prodigal son, a young man decided to move from the love, comfort, and the security of home in order to "enjoy life" and do as he pleased in a far away country. He ended up living among pigs and eventually decided to come home and was received with joy. Just like the biblical prodigal son's father, God is always waiting with open arms to forgive and to love us. With Him is where we belong.

If you are reading this text and are not born again, take it as no coincidence. God wants to give you a new beginning, to make you righteous through Jesus Christ, and He promises an eternal life. He wants to come and dwell inside you and give your life meaning and purpose. Furthermore, you will boast a new and powerful identity as a child of God—the one that if you realize it will enable you to live a fulfilling, victorious, and blessed life in this earth. All you have to do is to be born again; God made it simple so that all of us can do it.

> If you confess with your mouth, "Jesus is Lord," and believe in your heart that God raised him from the dead, you will be saved. For it is with your heart that you believe and are justified, and it is with your mouth that you confess and are saved.
>
> —Romans 10:9–10

Based on the above scripture, and if you feel a stirring inside of you to be born again, I encourage you to say the following prayer out loud. After that you will be saved or born again.

Lord Jesus, I invite You into my life. I believe that You died for me and that You rose again. I give You my life, and in exchange I receive Yours. I am tired of living life my own way. Thank You for forgiving my sins and giving me a brand-new start. I pray in the name of Jesus. I believe I am now saved.

Congratulations! If you prayed this prayer, you are now a child of God. He has great things in store for you— privileges and blessings that only His children can enjoy.

A New Beginning with Christ; We Have Been Forgiven

We all love new beginnings; that is why we look forward to new seasons. With Jesus, every day has the potential for a new beginning, refreshment, restoration, and new energy. If you are a born-again child of God, your sins which separated you from Him have been forgiven. We all love being forgiven by people that we offend: friends, family members, strangers, colleagues, neighbors, and the like. Offenses and unforgiveness tend to hurt relationships causing them to regress, stagnate, and even deteriorate bitterly. But when we humble ourselves and ask for forgiveness, relationships can be restored because that offense is dealt with and removed out of the way.

However, there is a difference between the way people forgive and the way God forgives us. People may forgive but they do not necessarily forget. They can genuinely forgive, let go of the offense, and even restore a relationship; but sometimes it takes an event, person, or place to trigger the remembrance of the past offense albeit forgiven. As a coping mechanism, we have a tendency of pushing to the back of our minds or subconscious painful or traumatic events. That is just human nature, and it's our natural way of coping and surviving. But God not only forgives, He has the supreme ability of forgetting our sins too! That alone ought to be liberating. Isaiah 43:25 tells us, "I, even I, am he who blots out your transgressions, for my own sake, and remembers your sins no more."

It took the spotless blood of Jesus Christ for the offense of sin that was blocking man's free access to the almighty God to be absolved and atoned once and for all. Adam and Eve hid from God after sinning because sin tends to block our free access to God. God hates sin. David says,

> Blessed is he whose transgressions are forgiven, whose sins are covered. Blessed is the man whose sin the Lord does not count against him and in whose spirit is no deceit.
>
> —PSALM 32:1–2

When we accept Jesus as our Lord and Savior, all our past sins are forgiven—all of them. It does not matter what we did or how horrific or gruesome it was; the powerful blood of Jesus forgives all sins as if they were never done. That is why being born again gives us a fresh and liberated new start. All that weight from our sins is taken away and we can begin to enjoy a fellowship, friendship, and relationship with God with a free conscience. We are even worthy to serve Him!

> From Jesus Christ, who is the faithful witness, the firstborn from the dead, and the ruler of the kings of the earth. To him who loves us and has freed us from our sins by his blood, and has made us to be a kingdom and priests to serve his God and Father—to him be the glory and power for ever and ever! Amen.
>
> —REVELATION 1:5–6

Therefore, we have to stop believing lies from the devil and rebuke him when he keeps reminding us of our past mistakes (he does that through other people and our own thoughts). Instead, we have to remind him of 2 Corinthians 5:17, "Therefore, if anyone is in Christ, he is a new creation, the old has gone, the new has come."

Stop being bound by the sins of your past which were forgiven when you accepted Jesus as your Lord and Savior and begin your brand-new life with Him in freedom. You have been set free! Cease living your life feeling guilty and burdened by your past mistakes; after all there is nothing you can do about them. But Jesus has set you free from condemnation and has lifted the weight of your sin from your shoulders. You were going to be accountable for your sins on judgment day but upon salvation, your record was wiped clean by Christ's blood giving you a fresh and new beginning. Allow the Spirit of God in you to lead you into all truth and in the process set you free.

> Therefore, there is now no condemnation for those
> who are in Christ Jesus, because through Christ
> Jesus the law of the Spirit of life set me free from
> the law of sin and death.
>
> —Romans 8:1–2

We should cooperate with the Holy Spirit as He transforms us so that we become more and more like Jesus instead of wasting time looking back and feeling sorry for ourselves and beating ourselves for what we did. Apologize if you have to, set things straight, and do what you have to do to repair the harm or damage you did; but ultimately know that God has forgiven and set you free through Christ.

Yes, We Are Free Indeed!

It is one thing knowing what the Word of God says about us and another thing actually believing and applying it into our day-to-day lives. We have to know that the Word of God is the truth. You cannot change the truth. You might not understand it or you might find it hard to believe, but the truth, any truth, never changes. Therefore, it is up to us to change the way we think, our views, and the way we feel and start believing the truth until it becomes established in us; that's when it will truly liberate us.

John 8:36 says, "So if the Son sets you free, you will be free indeed." Note that the Word says it's only when the Son sets you free that you are really free. Real freedom does not come through the justice system, the counselor, or any self-help material; it comes through the one and only Savior, our Lord Jesus Christ. You can have this freedom in the midst of a controlling, oppressive, domineering, tyrannical atmosphere.

Where else can you get this kind of freedom? Do you know that as much as it is possible to live in a repressive environment and still have this kind of freedom, it is also equally possible to live in an independent, democratic, and liberated setting but still feel bound and subjugated on the inside? As the children of God, we have been given freedom by Christ who has come to dwell in us. No matter what is happening on the outside and, indeed, regardless of our past, we are free. God sets us free from generational curses and bondages. It is only the blood of Jesus that has the power to break every kind of bondage in this world. It doesn't matter if the bondage has been passed on from generation to generation; the blood of Jesus transcends all that. We are no longer prisoners or captives of our past. Jesus says,

> "The Spirit of the Lord is on me, because he has
> anointed me to preach good news to the poor. He
> has sent me to proclaim freedom for the prisoners
> and recovery of sight for the blind, to release the
> oppressed, to proclaim the year of the Lord's favor."
> —LUKE 4:18–19

Even a prisoner doing time in a maximum security facility can have this inner freedom and peace if they give their life to Jesus and be born again. God will forgive and forget their offense. He will take away their guilt and shame and give them a new identity. As far as God is concerned, that person is His child in whom the Holy Spirit has come to dwell. And, if they allow Him, He will transform them to be the best they could ever be. Also, God will give them peace and joy which has nothing to do with their restrictive environment. You see, God's perspective is different from ours, which is usually limited; He is almighty and sovereign and when He begins His work in us, He is not restricted by our past, whether bad or good. In another chapter we will discuss how even the "good" past can also be a stumbling block in our walk with God.

Chapter 3

WE HAVE BEEN SAVED BY GRACE

As born-again believers we have received the gift of eternal life because Christ died for us and took our place on the cross. He died for us while we were still deep in sin; He did not wait for us to straighten ourselves out first before He could reconcile us to God through His death.

> You see, at just at the right time, when we were still powerless, Christ died for the ungodly. Very rarely will anyone die for a righteous man, though for a good man someone might possibly dare to die. But God demonstrates his own love for us in this: While we were still sinners, Christ died for us.
>
> —Romans 5:6–8

He saved us by His grace. We did not deserve to be saved but His love for us made Him endure the pain, shame, and humiliation of the cross. We are not saved by our good works, individual effort, or through recommendation from somebody, but by His grace alone. No amount of great work no matter how noble could ever buy or qualify us for salvation. Any other doctrine which claims we can be saved any way other than by grace through faith is misleading, according to the Word of God.

> For it is by grace you have been saved, through faith—and this is not from yourselves, it is the gift of God—not by works, so that no one can boast.
>
> —EPHESIANS 2:8–9

Grace is unmerited favor, it is not earned; otherwise that's not grace at all. God loved us so much and wanted us to be reconciled to Him that He sent His only beloved Son down to earth to die on our behalf so we could belong to Him and receive the gift of eternal life. No longer are we under the law; it was done away with when Jesus died and rose again. We are now guided by the Holy Spirit who leads us into righteous living that pleases God.

> The law was added so that the trespass might increase. But where sin increased, grace increased all the more, so that, just as sin reigned in death, so also grace might reign through righteousness to bring eternal life through Jesus Christ our Lord.
>
> —ROMANS 5:20–21

With grace there are no small sins or big sins; all of them are covered by the same blood of Jesus. Your sins may have been different from mine; but by the grace of God, we were both given a new identity and "accepted in the beloved" (Eph. 1:6, KJV).

CHRISTIANS ARE MEANT TO LIVE BY GRACE

God does not stop at saving and adopting us as His children by grace. He continues to be gracious toward us in our day-to-day lives; guiding us, providing for us, and protecting us. He shows us mercy and compassion and in every circumstance, He is right there beside us and He wants us to lean on Him and find help in times of need. All we have to do is to surrender all aspects of our lives to Him and trust Him to take care of us. The way we live our lives should manifest that we have the life of Christ in us, which enables us to do what we are meant to do and be able to endure difficult times. We have been given the Holy Spirit and He strengthens us from the inside so that we handle outside life situations with His divine ability. We cease to rely on our own strengths, wisdom, carnal desires, and head knowledge. If we do that, the Bible says we will be sons of God truly, "because those who are led by the Spirit of God are sons of God" (Rom. 8:14).

Sons of God are mature. They know who they are in Christ and they have no confidence in their flesh. Hence, they allow themselves to be led by God's Spirit and they are the ones who live successful, peaceful, and prosperous lives. They do not make life decisions based on feelings alone because they know that these change from time to time; but their Lord never changes. Hebrews 13:8 says, "Jesus is the same yesterday and today and forever." Therefore, they believe that whatever life throws at them, God's grace is always there to sustain them.

We should know that God cares about everything that happens to us and in whatever we do. He does not want us to drown or be overwhelmed by life. He knows our weaknesses and limitations and wants to help us where we struggle. His Word in Hebrews 4:16 says, "Let us then approach the throne of grace with confidence, so that we may receive mercy and find grace to help us in our time of need."

Whenever you feel like your life is full of struggle and is requiring more effort from you than you can give, or whenever you are left weary and worn out, check and see if you are allowing the Holy Spirit to lead you and if you are receiving God's grace. Jesus never promised an easy life without trials or challenges; but He promises His presence and strength in the midst of them. He will not always remove from our lives things that torment us and bring us discomfort, but He will give us the power to endure instead of falling apart.

The apostle Paul at one time had an agonizing problem that he asked God three times to remove. In 2 Corinthians 12:9 he says, "But he said to me, 'My grace is sufficient for you, for my power is made perfect in weakness.' Therefore I will boast all the more gladly about my weaknesses, so that God's power may rest on me."

God may not always move exactly when we want Him to, neither will He give us everything we want all the times; but He will never abandon us and He will be forever present giving us a shoulder to lean on when we need it the most. That is why our relationship with Him should never be based only on what He can do for us.

We fellowship with Him because we love Him, and He is our Father whom we hold in reverence; and His decisions are always right even if we may not always understand them.

If we live under God's grace, we will always be satisfied and fulfilled in life no matter what our circumstances are like. We won't be yoyo Christians, who are happy and praise God because things are going well in life and then sad, complaining, and disgruntled when they are not so good. Paul discovered the key to a contented life whether or not his needs were being met. Here are his thoughts written to the church of Philippi in regards to their gifts to him:

> I am not saying this because I am in need, for I have learned to be content whatever the circumstances. I know what it is to be in need, and I know what it is to have plenty. I have learned the secret of being content in any and every situation, whether well fed or hungry, whether living in plenty or in want. I can do everything through him who gives me strength.
>
> —PHILIPPIANS 4:11–13

This is one area we as the children of God can disarm the enemy's tactics in our lives. Whatever he brings to us intending to rattle and steal our peace and joy, we can respond by shifting our attention to Jesus and trusting that He will take care of us in a way only He can.

Many Christians genuinely hate sin and desire to live holy and righteous lives as the children of God. Most of the times we know the right things to do but unfortunately we allow the flesh to get the better of us. If we try pleasing God with our human strength only, we will fail; but if we are guided by the Holy Spirit, we will be able to overcome the flesh and do God's will.

> May the God of peace, who through the blood of the eternal covenant brought back from the dead our Lord Jesus, that great shepherd of the sheep, equip you with everything good for doing his will, and may he work in us what is pleasing to him, through Jesus Christ, to whom be glory for ever and ever. Amen.
>
> —Hebrews 13:20–21

Chapter 4

ONLY JESUS CAN MAKE US WHOLE

WITH SO MUCH going on around the world, aren't we blessed and privileged to be God's children? This is our true identity—who we are first and foremost. Being children of God, who created heaven and earth, is just priceless. We should have stability, security, and fulfillment because our Father reigns and is in control of everything.

> For in Christ all the fullness of the Deity lives in bodily form, and you have been given fullness in Christ who is the head over every power and authority.
>
> —COLOSSIANS 2:9–10

Whatever void was there in our lives before we received Jesus in our lives was filled with power from on high. We are no longer at the mercy of the forces and powers of darkness; neither are we defenseless and vulnerable, because He who conquered hell lives in us. According to 1 John 4:4, "You, dear children, are from God and have overcome them, because the one who is in you is greater than the one who is in the world."

When we see the chaos happening in the world today,

the more we realize the human need for salvation. There are people looking to fill that inner void with all sorts of things; drugs, sexual immorality and perversions, strange reality shows, and the like. All these things and others may provide some pleasure and purpose in the short-term, but they can never ever fill that inner void and hunger. Even in Jesus' time there were people who followed Him because He had miraculously fed them all with bread and they wanted more of it. And He directed them to Himself, because that is what they really needed.

> Then Jesus declared, "I am the bread of life. He who comes to me will never go hungry, and he who believes in me will never be thirsty."
>
> —JOHN 6:35

Sometimes we think maybe if we get lots of money, find a partner in life, get a degree, or whatever we define as achievement, then we will be content and fulfilled. All these things are good, but as soon as we achieve them we may be shocked to realize that we are still empty on the inside. It is only when we are satisfied in the inner man that we can truly be complete and made whole. All the other things we desire may pacify for a while, but with time that hunger and thirst will return again. You cannot satisfy a spiritual need with something physical. In a quest to find meaning in life, people experiment and engage in all kinds of things which unfortunately end in self-destruction and even draw them further from God.

> The acts of the sinful nature are obvious: sexual immorality, impurity and debauchery: idolatry and witchcraft; hatred, discord, jealousy, fits of rage, selfish ambition, dissensions, factions and envy; drunkenness, orgies and the like. I warn you, as I did before, that those who live like this will not inherit the kingdom of God.
>
> —GALATIANS 5:19–21

Who does all these things except someone who is searching for something in life and who is frustrated, confused, and desperate, and who is disappointed when they fail to attain it? It appears the more we search for meaning and purpose in places and people other than Jesus, the more self-destructive and low we get.

Chapter 5

GOD'S SPIRIT GUIDES US TO LIVE OUT OUR TRUE IDENTITIES

WHEN YOU KNOW that after being born again your identity is now in Christ, you will be motivated to live a life that He wants you to have. You will not be satisfied with just cruising through life aimlessly, accepting whatever comes your way and being a victim of circumstances. Jesus Christ died and rose again. When He ascended to heaven, His work here on earth was done. He conquered all life's challenges for you and me so that we will live this life on earth to the full. The devil knows this and that is not want he wants for God's children. He works hard to ensure that we do not realize the power of our Christian identity in our everyday lives, and he desires to lead us into the way of destruction, struggle, and death. Jesus says,

> "The thief comes only to steal and kill and destroy;
> I have come that they may have life, and have it to
> the full."
>
> —JOHN 10:10

We all need some kind of guidance when embarking on a journey we are not familiar with. A wise traveler will use a map to direct him in his unknown journey; whereas a fool will just set off, thereby risking getting lost along the way and wandering into dangerous territory. We do not always know what lies ahead in our lives; we sometimes wish we did so that we could be well prepared to deal with it. But don't you think there are some things that will right off petrify you if you knew beforehand they were going to happen? However, Jesus knows we cannot make it successfully on our own. He declares,

> "I will not leave you orphans; I will come to you. Before long, the world will not see me anymore, but you will see me. Because I live, you also will live. On that day you will realize that I am in my Father, and you are in me, and I am in you."
> —John 14:18–20

As born-again believers we have been given the Holy Spirit to provide us with guidance and steer us towards the right direction in our walk with God and in life. As God's children we need the wisdom to know the difference between the facts of this life and God's truth. They are not always the same, neither do they have the ultimate similar effects in our lives; therefore, it is imperative that we be careful what we choose and allow to guide our actions.

If we examine our individual lives at any given time, we will honestly find areas in which we come short, some flaws and weaknesses. Those would be facts, just like when you have a physical illness, born again or not, something will not be functioning well in your body and that will be a fact. When your marriage is having some problems or when you have lost your job, in all these circumstances you cannot deny that something is amiss; otherwise that will be deception on your part.

Facts are not always negative, they can also be positive. The fact is there are some people who are doing well, successful, or gifted in life whether or not they are born again. You can have great academic achievement, excel in sports, and have an advancing career even if you have never said a single prayer or set foot in a church, right? But you see, you cannot base your life on and be guided by the facts of life only. How many times have we messed up after making decisions based on our wisdom and intelligence?

There are some things in life that are beyond our control and others are just unpredictable. Some things will change on us without a warning, just when we were sure we had them all figured out. Gifts and natural talent cannot be the basis of guiding and living one's life. They serve their purpose and are actually good, as they can enrich our lives and others, but they cannot be the compass for life. Don't you know of intelligent, gifted or talented people with broken lives? Facts, though facts, just like feelings, can change at anytime, but the truth never changes. Jesus says,

> "But when he, the Spirit of truth, comes, he will guide you into all truth. He will not speak of his own; he will speak only what he hears, and he will

tell you what is yet to come. He will bring glory
to me by taking from what is mine and making it
known to you."

—John 16:13–14

God is the one with the perfect plan for our lives. We know He has good plans for each and every one of us; but unless we yield to His Spirit, how will we know? I am not referring to His promises we can all find from reading the Bible; I mean the specific plan and purpose for your life. It would be a tragedy if we go through life never having discovered what God's personal plan is for us as individuals. We will still go to heaven when we die; but we are meant to live purposeful and significant lives on this earth too. God is our maker; He knows how we are meant to function efficiently. It therefore makes sense to permit Him to show us the way we ought to live if we want optimal performance in our lives.

His Spirit will guide, teach, comfort, warn, and advocate for us because He knows things that we don't. People can say they know you, especially those close to you, but no one can ever know you the way God does. There are some things God wants to do in our lives that we will never know or experience unless we are in tune with the Spirit. If we are not careful, just like the people in the world, if we are not led by the Spirit we may miss out on God's blessings in our lives because we will never find out what they are. For example: It's like having a relative die and leave you an inheritance that for some reason you never get to know about. You would continue living in lack and want when you should have been living in abundance.

God is a Spirit; therefore, He will want to guide and speak to us through our spirits. The apostle Paul was led by the Spirit in such a way that at times he would be warned against going into certain towns for his own safety. I believe by the time he eventually died, his work here on earth was done. God wants to be involved in every area of our lives today also. Even in this high tech fast world we live in today, He will lead us. He is able to guide our careers, businesses, and families; and our part is to listen to His voice and promptings. His mind and intentions will be revealed to our spirits as the children of God.

> However, as it is written: No eye has seen, no ear has heard, no mind has conceived what God has prepared for those who love him—but God has revealed it to us by his Spirit. The Spirit searches all things, even the deep things of God. For who among men knows the thoughts of a man's spirit within him? In the same way no one knows the thoughts of God except the Spirit of God. We have not received the spirit of the world but the Spirit who is from God, that we may understand what God has freely given us.
>
> —1 CORINTHIANS 2:9–12

Chapter 6

WHO WE ARE NEVER LETS GO

As I mentioned before, I was raised in poverty. My father died when we were young, leaving our unemployed mother to take care of us. At eleven years old, I was the eldest of four kids when he passed. Our mother struggled to feed and clothe us and pay for our education. We did not own a house; we shared with extended family from my father's side. After his death we were no longer welcome. During his illness I remember seeing him cry when he knew he was going to die.

I remember praying for him to be healed. Every night my family would gather and pray for his healing, but I particularly prayed for him on my own as we were close and I did not want him to die. I am not a soccer fan now, but back then I enjoyed listening to soccer on the radio with him and going together to watch live matches. He was very keen in helping me with my homework, and he just enjoyed teaching me stuff. As a result, I did well in school.

When he died, I was shattered and I felt like my whole world has collapsed. Life became dark and meaningless. Amidst all this emotional pain and confusion, I found myself at an early age looking after my younger siblings as our mother tried to make a living for us. I did all the cooking, laundry, cleaning, and my schoolwork on top of that. Furthermore, we were ill-treated by our relatives and they rarely helped us. Actually they physically and emotionally abused us. They could afford some luxuries and always had plenty of food, but they rarely shared with us. Their used clothes they gave to the other kids in the neighborhood. They threw their leftover food and they shouted and yelled at us. Sometimes they would even send us to the shops when it was dark for something like a bar of chocolate.

Mind you, we were still grieving for our father. We felt crushed, powerless and dejected. That was a painful experience for all of us that I personally felt heartbroken at that age. I missed my father terribly. Life was just so hard, yet at the same time I still had to work hard at school because my mother was a firm believer on the importance of getting a good education. Eventually we were threatened with eviction even though my mother was still paying rent. We tried to find affordable accommodation, but the only place we could afford had a reputation for drug use, prostitution, and other sleazy activities. I was terrified and my mother was scared, but she was running out of choices. The place was a low income residence. Some of the people there were unemployed and they relied on government benefits whereas others sustained themselves by whatever means necessary.

We had already been given a date to move out or risk being thrown out on the street. People came up with all kinds of suggestions to my mother: "Why don't you find a man and remarry someone who will look after you and your kids?" Or, "Why don't you distribute your kids amongst your relatives and start your own life afresh?" The most ridiculous was a suggestion for me to marry one of the young teachers in my school. He would take care of us until I reached an age when he could lawfully take me as his wife. I was aghast, shocked, and repulsed! My mother flat out refused.

She kept telling us kids that God will take of us. And He did; we were given a place to stay in our church premises by our pastors. We were not required to pay rent; therefore, my mother had some money available for school fees and uniforms.

When I look back now, in a way, literally living in church helped me to grow closer to God. Church activities and services where happening in my doorstep, therefore, I could not help it but be actively involved. I started attending the youth group when I was fifteen years old, and that's when I got saved. In retrospect I can see that God was orchestrating my life to teach me how to trust and rely on Him by what I had to go through. The Bible says in Romans 8:28, "And we know that in all things God works for the good of those who loves him, who have been called according to his purpose."

I have learned that God uses every situation in our lives to reveal His glory to us. Sometimes He allows us to go through the fire so that when we do get to the other side, we would be much stronger and chiseled than before. However, we may not always see it that way when we are experiencing the actual painful and difficult circumstances.

Take me for instance; as much as I was grateful for the church accommodation and appreciated the pastors for saving us from homelessness, I was embarrassed at living in a church. The building was in between a main road on one side and a school pathway on the other side. As a result, all students and teachers went past it and they knew the reason my family stayed there was because we were poor and on the verge of homelessness when we were rescued. Unbeknownst to me, that was the ideal environment for me to attend church more and end up being saved as a result.

You see how the devil tries to deceive and blind us and keep us from appreciating and being thankful for what God is doing in our lives? God blesses us and delivers us in a manner that we did not expect, but we somehow find reasons to be disgruntled instead of being grateful.

The children of Israel were delivered from their tormentor Pharaoh; God sent them fresh manna from heaven daily, but they began complaining and even looked down on the manna. They started yearning for things like garlic, onions, and leeks that they used to enjoy in Egypt. In place of focusing on their journey to the Promised Land and praising God for setting them free, they murmured and complained about minor details and inconveniences. They lost sight of the bigger picture of what God was doing in their lives. They were sidetracked from considering where God had taken them from, what He was doing and preparing them for, and ultimately where He was taking them to.

Oh, how I can totally relate to that! I was ashamed of living in a church building, ashamed that we did not have a normal house, and I completely lost sight that God had provided us with a free roof over our heads. We lived in peace and had no one ill-treating us. We had pastors and fellow church members who loved us and provided for us. We practically lived in an atmosphere of praise and worship; but check out the trivial issues that bothered me.

God knew what He was doing. He had a plan and purpose for my life; and according to Jeremiah 29:11, it was for good and not for evil. Everything was working out together for good; but at that time I was ignorant, young, and clueless.

Keep Your Eyes on the Big Picture

As born-again believers, it is crucial to realize who we are in Christ, recognize that God has a future and a destiny for us, and live surrendered lives and let Him be in control. Otherwise the devil will distract our attention to focus on situations present instead of where God plans to take us. The deceiver aims to divert our focus from the main picture. There are promises of God waiting to be fulfilled in our lives, our rightful inheritance as sons of God and joint heirs with Jesus Christ.

Knowing that we have been saved from eternal unquenchable fire but will live forever in eternal love, peace, and joy ought to make us embrace each day with hope and a feeling of security. As Christians we should have this internal assurance and confidence of who we are and mature from being yoyo Christians whom the devil can play like a fiddle. Jesus Christ is our solid rock on which we stand; therefore, we are unshakeable, firm, and solid and should not be tossed to and fro. He is our everything. Our lives should be grounded and rooted in Him alone. In the Book of Acts 17:28, the apostle Paul says, "'For in him we live and move and have our being.' As some of your own poets have said, 'We are his offspring.'"

We have to be moved by who we are in Christ and not by our situations, and so avoid being at the mercy of the devil's manipulations and deceit. You see, stuff will always happen in this world and in life, but it is up to us to change our perspective and the way we see things. Jesus prepared and equipped His disciples (and us) for what was in the world before He ascended to heaven. He says,

> "I have told you these things, so that in me you may have peace. In this world you will have trouble. But take heart! I have overcome the world."
>
> —JOHN 16:33

Regardless of what happens in life, if we have been born again, we are always overcomers and more than conquerors because the One who overcame and conquered lives in us. Children of God who have chosen to follow and trust in Him must wake up each morning knowing that God is in control of their lives and that

His eyes are forever on them. He is always watching what is happening in our lives and always listens when we cry out to Him.

> The eyes of the Lord are on the righteous and his ears are attentive to their prayer, but the face of the Lord is against those who do evil.
>
> —1 PETER 3:12

MY LIFE CHANGED FOR THE BETTER WHEN I REALIZED MY IDENTITY

As mentioned before, I was born again in a youth service when I was fifteen years old. By then my family had accommodation, but my mother still struggled to make ends meet. At that time I was in high school; and because I studied hard, I was always in the first class throughout and was doing well academically. This meant my mother was working extra hard to raise money for school and to put food on the table. During the day I would help her by selling fruits and vegetables around the block, and at night I would study and do my homework. I was determined to pass, secure myself a future, and help my mother financially and ease her struggles.

I remember nights when I would go into the main church hall and pray at length. I prayed for my family; for God to have mercy on us, to change our lives, and to provide for us. And sometimes I would just cry out in anger and ask Him, "Why?" There were days when I was sent back from school because my school fees were not paid up. That used to break my mother's heart. I remember seeing her crying and praying as she felt hopeless. This was a woman who was unwavering in her quest for us to be educated and be able to break the cycle of poverty. She used to put on a brave face for us kids; but because I was older, I could see her ache underneath it all.

One particular night I remember vividly; I was on my knees in tears in the church hall. Loudly, frankly, and clearly I told God I was tired of poverty and struggling. I cried to Him and reminded Him that His Word stated that He was a God who looked after the widows and the fatherless. I reminded Him of Psalm 10:14, which declares:

> But you, O God, do see trouble and grief; you consider it to take it in hand. The victim commits himself to you; and you are the helper of the fatherless.

Of all the heartfelt prayers I have ever prayed in my life, I will always particularly remember that one. I challenged God and reminded Him of His promises to His children. My heart was filled with so much pain and anguish. I told God that I had had enough. I reminded Him that I was His child and therefore, my life deserved to be better. I recall sobbing so much that my whole body literally shook. Eventually I just lay there on the floor feeling spent, having reached a point where there was nothing else I could do. All this time God was listening and watching me. I recollect suddenly feeling this overwhelming rush of peace and calm envelop me like a blanket. It was like a rush of warm oil all over my body.

That was my first experience of God's physical demonstration of power in my life. It was like God was confirming that, "Yes," I am His child, He loved me, He was right there with me, and everything was going to be all right. I slept very peaceful that night. A new resilience and inner strength was borne in me that night.

Is it not amazing that God usually shows up when we have reached the end of our strengths and ability? When we have worn ourselves out, have done all we can, and finally decide to surrender to Him, that's when He begins to act on our behalf and release His power. It would save us a lot of pain and time if we could just decide to trust God and seek His omnipotent guidance in the very beginning. God releases His power in areas where we feel weak and powerless when we reach the end of our tether.

> That is why, for Christ's sake, I delight in weaknesses, in insults, in hardships, in persecutions, in difficulties. For when I am weak, then I am strong.
> —2 Corinthians 12:10

My mother eventually got the money for my final examinations by God's grace. God provided for us and answered our prayers in that hopeless hour of need. God is very resourceful and creative; He knows everything and owns everything and can change anything at anytime. That is why His Word says in 1 Corinthians 1:25, "For the foolishness of God is wiser than man's wisdom, and the weakness of God is stronger than man's strength."

My life changed from that moment onward beginning with a fifteen-year-old sobbing and reaching out to God and crying, "God help me; I am your child and I deserve better." At that stage in my walk with God, that is all I knew about my identity as a Christian; but God delivered me anyway.

God can do that for you too. He can set you free from whatever is oppressing and hindering you from moving forward and enjoying your life. If we are born-again believers who are conscious of what it means both in this life and in the one to come, we will be confident in the power of our God-given identity. We will believe we are what the Word says we are, expect to receive what the Word says is rightfully ours, and be bold to do what God says we can do.

According to Zechariah 4:6, it is "not by might nor by power, but by my Spirit, says the LORD Almighty." The importance of trusting in God and being led by His Spirit can never be overemphasized. The greater One who dwells in the inner man is by far greater than any challenge we may ever face on the outside. Moreover His peace and joy will take us through the difficult times. We are strong from the inside.

Chapter 7

TREASURE YOUR IDENTITY

W HEN YOU POSSESS something of value, you esteem it, watch over it, and make sure it is not tampered with. A thief comes to steal something of worth and significance. He breaks into a bank because he is after the money and other valuables that are kept in the vault. Likewise, a thief breaks into an art gallery for the paintings, which is what is of most value in there.

Similarly, with you as a believer, the thief (devil) wants to steal your true identity from you. How does he do that? Well, if he can get you not to appreciate and realize who you are in Christ, he would have succeeded in making you live a purposeless, defeated, unstable, and confused life on earth. He wants to keep the truth about who you really are from you. The devil will feed you with his lies, and you will believe whatever the world says and thinks about you.

Of course you will still go to heaven because we are saved by grace and not by our works, but Jesus also died so we could live triumphant and fruitful lives in this lifetime too. We do that by realizing, treasuring, and living out our true identity in Christ.

The Word of God Is the Truth

To be successful and in order to reap the benefits of our identity in Christ, we have to renew our minds with the Word of God.

> Do not conform any longer to the pattern of this world, but be transformed by the renewing of your mind. Then you will be able to approve and test what God's will is—his good, pleasing and perfect will.
>
> —Romans 12:2

The world will conform us to its standard and way of life unless we renew our minds. The devil knows mind renewal is an important key to living victorious everyday lives; therefore, he will do whatever it takes to make sure we do not fully attain and grasp that. He is, among other things, a liar, a deceiver, and a master in distracting believers from realizing the power of their true identity. This easily happens when we do not have a solid foundation of our position in Christ in accordance with the Word of God.

It is important to note that upon salvation, it is our spirits that are changed and transformed when God's Spirit comes to live in us. Our minds and bodies remain the same way they were before. You will be born again but still have your same physique and same thoughts running through your mind. That is why some people feel guilty and frustrated when they continue behaving the same way they did before they got born again. Hence, we need the Word of God to cleanse and wash away all the debris that accumulated over the years until we are clean; when our minds are saturated by the powerful and living Word of God. We need Christ's perception and mind, and the Word of God is the source of that.

> For who has known the mind of the Lord that he
> may instruct him? But we have the mind of Christ.
> —1 CORINTHIANS 2:16

The mind of Christ is found in the Word, our faith in Christ grows from the Word, and therefore, we begin to make decisions based on the Word and not on our feelings. We discover from the Word of God who we are and how this impacts our lives. And it is also where we get a solid foundation of our position in Christ. Focusing and firmly believing in our position in Christ equips us as believers to deal with whatever condition we find ourselves in from God's perspective.

From our position in Christ we believe that whatever the Word of God says about any situation is the truth and never changes; therefore, any condition or situation is subject to change if it is not in line with God's Word and promises. From our position in Christ, we believe that whatever God says about us is the truth and if we have faith, it shall come to pass.

We believe also that our condition does not always reflect our true identity and therefore cannot determine our future and destiny. In the Bible, I believe, there are some people whose identity was stolen, if not momentarily, because they allowed the devil to deceive them. Unfortunate consequences resulted.

Samson's Stolen Identity

Samson, an Israelite, was conceived through God's divine intervention. His father, Manoah, had a wife who was infertile. It was at a time when the Israelites were being defeated by the Philistines because they had disobeyed God. They were being judged by God because of their disobedience, hence their defeat at war. An angel appeared to Manoah's wife, and told her what she needed to do in order to conceive a child whom God was going to use to deliver the people of Israel from the Philistines. One of the requirements was that the child should never shave his head all the days of his life. He was to be a Nazarite; which meant he was set apart and consecrated by God. This involved observing particular requirements like abstaining from certain foods and drinks.

As long as Samson remained consecrated, God was going to use him to defeat the Israelites who were tormenting His people. The Lord blessed Samson and His Spirit was upon his life such that he had tremendous victory and supernatural strength. At one point, he even used a jawbone of a dead donkey to kill a thousand Philistines all by himself (Judg. 15:15). During the time that he remained consecrated and had God's Spirit upon him, Samson was supernaturally strong and could not be subdued.

The Philistines were baffled as to the source of Samson's power. They did not know it was because of who he was; that he was chosen of God and endowed with His power. They became intent on finding out what was happening. Therefore, they paid Delilah money in return for information as to the secret to Samson's strength in order for them to be able to subdue him.

You see, we are up against a devil who is relentless; he goes to great lengths and uses all means necessary to strip us of the power of our identity. For as long as we are careless with and do not value our precious identity, he will divert, deceive, and distract us into living powerless lives devoid of anointing, purpose, and influence. This is what happened to Samson; as soon as he revealed to Delilah the source of his strength, God's anointing and power immediately left him. Three times Samson had lied to Delilah as to the reason why he had tremendous strength. But Delilah did not give up; she pestered and manipulated him until he gave in. This is how it happened:

> With such nagging she prodded him day after day until he was tired to death. So he told her everything. "No razor has ever been used on my head," he said, "because I have been a Nazarite set apart to God since birth. If my head were shaved, my strength would leave me, and I would become as weak as any other man." When Delilah saw that he had told her everything, she sent word to the rulers of the Philistines, "Come back once more; he has told me everything." So the rulers of the Philistines returned with the silver in their hands. Having put him to sleep on her lap, she called a man to shave off the seven braids of his hair, and so began to subdue him. And his strength left him. Then she called, "Samson, the Philistines are upon you!" He woke from his sleep and thought, "I'll go

out as before and shake myself free." But he did not know that the LORD had left him. Then the Philistines seized him, gouged out his eyes and took him down to Gaza. Binding him with bronze shackles, they set him to grinding in the prison.

—JUDGES 16:16–21

What a tragic thing when we think we can still be victorious, not knowing that God's power has left us. But our God is a God of second chances, mercy, and forgiveness. When Samson realized what had happened, he cried to God for one more chance to defeat the Philistines. His hair had begun to grow again while in prison. God answered his prayers, and Samson unselfishly died with all the Philistines who had gathered for a performance and to gloat over him, not knowing God's power had been restored to him again. He had reestablished his purpose and reclaimed his identity in the Lord.

You too can make the decision today that you will realize you now belong to God, that you have been set apart, and that you have God's Spirit residing in you; therefore, you possess power over the evil one and the battles he may bring your way. Victory and triumph is assured all the times as long as God is with you.

DAVID'S CRY FOR THE HOLY SPIRIT

David loved the Lord and spent most of his time worshiping and writing psalms and hymns for Him. In 1 Samuel 13:14, God proclaimed that David was a man after His own heart. Therefore, not surprisingly, God chose him to be the king of the Israelites.

How marvelous are the plans and purposes God has for us when we put Him first and seek Him diligently! It does not matter what obstacles we may encounter in order to fulfill our destinies, as long as God is with us, He will provide the breakthroughs.

Unfortunately, as much as David loved the Lord and his heart was right toward Him, he was also a human being subject to the same temptations as the rest of us. In a moment of weakness and poor judgment, he gave in to temptation and committed adultery. The day he slept with Bathsheba, Uriah's wife, David was not even supposed to be home. He was in the wrong place at the wrong time. In that situation, we become vulnerable and become more likely to give in to temptation than if we had remained in God's plans. Believers who are led by the Spirit of God are much more able to resist temptation because the Spirit seeks to please God whereas the flesh seeks to give in to its passions and desires leading to sin and trouble.

In Matthew 4:1–11 it tells us that Jesus overcame temptation in the desert because He was led by the Spirit. He was meant to be there, fasting and praying for forty days and forty nights in the presence of God. The devil tried to entice Him with various worldly temptations, but Jesus did not succumb because the Spirit was with Him all the time. Jesus reached a point where He had to sharply rebuke the devil when he dared suggest that Jesus bow down and worship him. We can only imagine how intense the experience was for Him because afterwards God sent angels to comfort Him.

Unfortunately David stayed at home that evening when he was meant to be leading the army in battle as was required of him according to 2 Samuel 11:1–4. Not only did he commit adultery, he further went on to kill Uriah so he could have his wife whom he had impregnated. If David had not deviated from God's plan that day, maybe he would not have seen Uriah's wife bathing and opened a door that led to his subsequent problems. Instead of doing what he was supposed to be doing, he found himself with time in his hands; maybe he was bored even. When he decided to get out of bed and stroll around, that's when he saw Bathsheba. The Bible says she was a very beautiful woman. Even after enquiring around and being told she was somebody's wife, that did not stop David from lusting after her. He just had to have her.

God was not pleased with David's actions and the pain and suffering he had caused. He sent Nathan the prophet to tell him about the judgment that was to befall him as a result. David was devastated! Although he had sinned, he still loved God and therefore longed for forgiveness and the restoration of their relationship.

God Cares for the Inner Man

Psalm 51 is David's heartfelt cry for God to forgive him and purify his heart once again. His heart was heavy with sorrow and grief, and he knew that his sin had distanced him from God. This was a man who delighted in God's presence very much, always praising, worshiping and marveling at His greatness. He had tasted the goodness of the Lord and he knew there was nothing like it. He also knew that as a result of his sin he could not freely enter God's presence as he did before.

However, he was also aware that it was only God who could forgive and restore him from the inside. We tend to focus on outside appearances and on the tangible things, but God looks at the heart, the innermost being. In Psalms 51:6, David says, "Surely you desire truth in the inner parts, you teach me wisdom in the inmost place." Hence he yearned for God to renew his spirit and make him right on the inside again.

One of the toughest challenges in life is trying to conquer the internal war and to quiet the unrest deep within us. These have nothing to do with physical strength and prowess. David had accomplished many outward victories, both while he was still a shepherd in the fields and in the battlefield. He was strong and powerful; the dead bear, lion, and Goliath are proof of that.

However, the spiritual, moral, and mental anguish that ensued after his sin was just too much for him to bear. He was in an internal war. Fortunately he knew that only God had the ability to deliver him, set him free, and heal his innermost wounds. David had his priorities in order; he recognized what was of most importance in his life. Although he was a powerful and wealthy ruler, the only thing he cried to God *not* to take away from him was the Holy Spirit and then he asked for the restoration of their relationship.

He was aware that was where the power of his existence and purpose emanated from. Who he was, what he had done and accomplished; all his victories and even his joy were a result of God's presence in his life. God had taken him from being a shepherd and made him into a mighty king of Israel. David didn't care about his vast fortunes and title; he so desperately wanted to be right with God again. Material possessions and other outside wealth perish; but inner wealth, which is righteousness, is forever. According to Paul, the inner man actually defies the laws of nature by being renewed while the outside is degenerating.

> Therefore we do not lose heart. Though outwardly we are wasting away, yet inwardly we are being renewed day by day. For our light and momentary troubles are achieving for us an eternal glory that far outweighs them all. So we fix our eyes not on what is seen, but what is unseen. For what is seen is temporary, but what is unseen is eternal.
> —2 CORINTHIANS 4:16–18

After this difficult time in his life when he experienced God's judgment, David also discovered how gracious, loving, and forgiving God is. God restored him and gave him a different kind of crown which outweighed any other. David expressed his joy:

> Praise the LORD, O my soul, and forget not all his benefits—who forgives all your sins and heals all your diseases, who redeems your life from the pit and crowns you with love and compassion, who satisfies your desires with good things so that your youth is renewed like the eagle's.
> —PSALM 103:2–5

PRIORITIZE GOD; HE WILL MEET YOUR PHYSICAL NEEDS TOO

God cares about all aspects of our lives; the spiritual, mental, physical, and the social. He wants us to be whole; therefore, as much as He desires for us to get it right spiritually first, He is still interested in meeting our other needs too. God yearns for us to set our priorities straight by putting Him first. And He promises that if we do that, then He will satisfy our other needs in this lifetime. We are already blessed by being His children, but He also wants to prosper us and make us successful in whatever we do. However, He wants to break the spirit of materialism and of seeking security and joy from tangible physical things when He has already given us the greatest gift we can ever receive: Jesus Christ.

Even if we never prosper materially and accumulate monetary and worldly riches, we should still be satisfied and fulfilled as long as we have a relationship with God. Jesus Christ died and rose again so that we could enjoy this relationship; therefore, all the other things really are nothing and just don't compare with the gift of eternal life. God wants us to love Him for who He is and not what He can do for us. Real peace and real joy is found from having an intimate and personal relationship with God, and not from all these other things. Jesus encourages us about prioritizing these things. In Matthew 6:33 He says, "But seek first his kingdom and his righteousness, and all these things will be given to you as well."

It is a pity when believers are caught up in chasing after accumulating possessions and wealth at the expense of seeking to draw nearer to God and developing a deeper and intimate relationship with Him. If we are going to be truly successful and fulfilled in life, then putting God first in our lives should become our lifestyle. Then, through faith, we will trust Him and believe that He will meet all our other needs. God wants to be prioritized in everything we do, we can't live our lives by worldly standards and try to fit Him in the convenient gaps and then call ourselves Christians. We need to choose and commit to what is most important in our lives—worldly desires or total surrender to God, we can't have both. The Bible says,

> No one can serve two masters. Either he will hate the one and love the other, or he will be devoted to the one and despise the other. You cannot serve both God and Money.
>
> —MATTHEW 6:24

Chapter 8

GOD NEVER GIVES UP ON US

WE ALL MAKE mistakes as believers. That does not necessarily mean that we do not love God anymore or have chosen the world over Him. It just means we are not perfect, that we are human, and that we are people. But Jesus, who is perfect and righteous, understands us and that is why He is constantly interceding for us. A mistake can be an opportunity to learn and grow and build our character. God does not give up on us because we have made mistakes or exercised bad judgment. He is a loving, patient, and forgiving Father. We should never let our past or present sins and mistakes hinder us from moving forward with God.

The devil takes advantage of these moments of weakness to weigh us down with guilt and self-loathing. He tells us we are unworthy of God's presence; and he wants us to believe that because we have sinned, God is disappointed with us and only judgment and punishment await us. He brings gloom and doom in these situations. But Jesus does not condemn us. He steps right into the situation and reminds us that nothing can separate us from His love. The apostle Paul says,

> Who will bring any charge against those whom God has chosen? It is God who justifies. Who is he that condemns? Christ Jesus, who died—more than that, who was raised to life—is at the right hand of God and is also interceding for us. Who shall separate us from the love of Christ? Shall trouble or hardship or persecution or famine or nakedness or danger or sword?
>
> —ROMANS 8:33–35

If you are a child of God and have made a mistake, God cannot condemn you; you have been bought by the blood of Jesus Christ. You now belong to Him, and His Spirit in you is proof of that. It's like Jesus is saying, "I died and paid a price for him; he is Mine. I understand what he is going through. I do not like what he did, but I will forgive him and continue loving him. All he needs to do is to repent." Whatever happens in life, good or bad, unjust or unfair, God will never stop loving us because of what happened at the cross. His love for us is just too great for us to fathom and nothing can ever change that. Paul continues by saying,

> No, in all these things we are more than conquerors through him who loved us. For I am convinced that neither death nor life, neither angels nor demons, neither the present not the future, nor any powers, neither height nor depth, nor anything else in all creation, will be able to separate us from the love of God that is in Christ our Lord Jesus our Lord.
>
> —ROMANS 8:37–39

His love is always there for us even when we have messed up so much and feel like we do not deserve it. Yes, He will chastise and discipline us but He will not withdraw His love from us just because we have sinned or made mistakes. This is a lie from the devil, the father of deception and lies.

WE HAVE BEEN GRANTED UNLIMITED ACCESS TO GOD

We have established that (1) Jesus died so that we could be reconciled to God and have a relationship and fellowship with Him, (2) He loves us, and (3) nothing can separate us from His love. It is written that when Christ died, the veil that separated us from God's divine presence was literally torn from the top to the bottom (see Matthew 27:50–51). This was done to give you and me unlimited access to our Father all the time and any time. We were given this direct access through the powerful blood of Jesus. The very last thing to happen before Jesus hung His head and died was the removal of this barrier between God's presence and us.

> The sun stopped shining. And the curtain of the temple was torn in two. Jesus called out with a loud voice, "Father, into you hands I commit my spirit." When he had said this, he breathed his last.
> —LUKE 23:45–46

Nothing should hinder us from entering God's presence and moving forward with Him. We can be as intimate with God as we want. It all depends on us; God is always waiting for us to take the first step toward Him. In His presence, as we fellowship with Him, we grow spiritually as He transforms us to be more like Jesus. In this place we find forgiveness, restoration, peace, and joy. God has provided us with everything we need; all we have to do is reach out in faith and receive it. And because of Jesus Christ, we can do that with boldness and confidence and without condemnation.

> Therefore, brothers, since we have confidence to enter the Most Holy Place by the blood of Jesus, by a new and living way opened for us through the curtain, that is, his body, and since we have a great priest over the house of God, let us draw near to God with a sincere heart in full assurance of faith, having our hearts sprinkled to cleanse us from a guilty conscience and having our bodies washed with pure water.
>
> —HEBREWS 10:19–22

It is common and natural to feel heavy in your spirit and soul, and guilty and condemned after sinning or even backsliding. But you do not have to stay that way. There is no sin too great that God cannot forgive if you genuinely and sincerely ask Him to. Do not fall into the enemy's trap by thinking that you have disappointed God so much that He does not want anything to do with you anymore. That is bondage; and we are not in bondage anymore. We are the children of grace. We do not have to labor for God's love and forgiveness. All He requires from you is a broken spirit and a confession that only He can truly save and restore you. According to Psalm 51:17,

"The sacrifices of God are a broken spirit; a broken and contrite heart, O God, you will not despise."

If only I had known this truth years back when I made a terrible mistake in my life. I was a born-again believer who loved God. When I made this mistake, I felt totally horrible, guilty, ashamed, and unworthy of God's presence and love. I had stopped going to church, I ceased studying the Word, and I began praying less and less. I could sense the devil was saying, "You have really blown it this time. You have really let God down. What kind of Christian are you?"

Those were the devil's lies from the pit of hell. He uses these unfortunate situations in our lives to attempt to draw us further from God through weighing us down with feelings of guilt and self-loathing. It's also an opportunity for him to attack our faith and make us question who we are as believers. It's in these vulnerable moments that he goes for the kill; when we are down. That is why we are cautioned in 1 Peter 5:8 to "be self-controlled and alert. Your enemy the devil prowls around like a roaring lion looking for someone to devour." It is so much easier for the devil to pounce on Christians when they are at their lowest point. We all know of fellow believers who took wrong steps and eventually ended up backsliding. Nothing good comes from the devil. When a believer is down, the devil comes to finish him off. But our Lord Jesus is merciful, compassionate, and He comes to comfort and uplift us when we are down and helpless. He is always willing to reach out in love and lift us out of our mess.

> Rend your heart and not your garments. Return to
> the Lord your God, for he is gracious and com-
> passionate, slow to anger and abounding in love,
> and he relents from sending calamity.
>
> —Joel 2:13

We should cease beating ourselves up and being ridden with guilt when we sin. We need to go back to our Father in brokenness and repentance. It's not about the nature or size of our sins; God loves and forgives us because of the price Jesus paid at the cross in order for us to be reconciled to Him. Therefore, it is never too late for any believer to go back to their first love. God never stops loving us despite what we do.

Chapter 9

GOD WANTS US TO LET GO OF THE "GOOD" PAST AS WELL

WHENEVER BELIEVERS MENTION leaving the past behind and moving forward with God, they tend to think about the bad past from which God delivered them. If we are to fully attain what God has in store for us as His children, we have to let go of *everything* from the past. It is easy to leave bad or painful things in the past. But it can be difficult to understand why we have to let go of some good stuff as well. You see, past achievements can become stumbling blocks in our walk with God. This is because we tend to be locked and frozen with awe at that moment in time when God is actually trying to take us to a greater place; a place where we can fulfill our destinies and give Him all the glory.

No past achievement, no matter how great or magnificent, can ever come close to comparing with the riches that are found in Christ Jesus. Paul says those things are nothing. This comes from a man, previously known as Saul, who had many achievements before his life-changing encounter with Jesus on the road to Damascus. In his letter to the Philippians, he advised them not to have any confidence in their flesh, in themselves, or in what they achieved in their own strength and power. He goes on to tell them that his past personal accomplishments gave him more reasons to boast than they had.

> I myself have reasons for such confidence. If anyone else thinks he has reasons to put confidence in the flesh, I have more: circumcised on the eighth day, of the people of Israel, of the tribe of Benjamin, a Hebrew of Hebrews; in regard to the law, a Pharisee; as for zeal, persecuting the church; as for legalistic righteousness, faultless. But whatever was my profit I now consider loss for the sake of Christ. What is more, I consider everything a loss compared to the surpassing greatness of knowing Christ Jesus my Lord, for whose sake I have lost all things. I consider them rubbish, that I may gain Christ.
>
> —PHILIPPIANS 3:4–8

Past achievements differ from person to person. For some these may be tied to their educational backgrounds, wealth, jobs, or prior associations. All of these are good and they serve their purpose in life. However, the question is: "Who are you when all these are stripped from you?" When we become born again, we should cease to be identified by them. We become Christians, which means "Christlike."

This is what should primarily define and identify us. Aspiring to be Christlike more and more through the working of the Holy Spirit and by the renewal of our minds by the Word of God is what leads us to our predestined destinies and living the life God intended for us to live from the very beginning. This is what makes us whole and fulfilled and brings meaning to life as God moves us from glory to glory.

Chapter 10

WE HAVE BEEN
PREDESTINED BY GOD

THERE IS NO single individual on the face of this earth who took God by surprise. Regardless of the circumstances surrounding our birth or conception, God knew each and every one of us way before we were even born. He operates from a much higher and different perspective than ours.

> "For my thoughts are not your thoughts, neither are your ways my ways," declares the LORD. "As the heavens are higher than the earth, so are my ways higher than your ways and my thoughts than your thoughts."
>
> —ISAIAH 55:8–9

God is always in ultimate control even though events may appear otherwise from our point of view. He knows everything before it happens. He is God Almighty; whether the good, the bad, the evil, or even the horrendous, nothing is hidden from Him.

No one should let how they were brought into this world define or label them. Their future in Christ is not necessarily tied to that. If your parents planned for and

69

anticipated your birth, praise God for that because He foreknew, approved, and loved you. Similarly, if you were conceived through unplanned or unfortunate circumstances, you should praise God too, for He also equally foreknew and approved of you. You are significant, unique, and special to Him.

You may have come unexpectedly or unplanned to the people involved, and you may have even been labeled a mistake; but that does not change how God sees and feels about you. Your existence did not catch Him unaware; therefore, He does not have to scratch His head and wonder what you will become; He already has a plan and purpose for your life. He knows and cares about the way you were conceived and the way you were brought up.

With Him, the end is better than the beginning. And He knows the end from the beginning. That's God perspective; He sees beyond our human and natural limitations. We sometimes make people outcasts and tend to judge them based on what *we* can see or comprehend. Sometimes we even make conclusions and predictions based on the knowledge we possess or lack. Unfortunately, these assumptions can be flawed, even presumptuous. Only God, by virtue of who He is, knows everything there is to know about an individual.

If we all understood that, there wouldn't be so much racism, intolerance, and prejudice against others, especially to those who are different from us. Someone once said racism is from the pit of hell. I totally agree. God made us all different because He likes the variety. Mind you, He had the option of making just one kind of people who all looked alike.

David had an in-depth revelation on how well, deep, and personal God really knows us. This knowledge ought to make all of us feel special, treasured, and significant, because that is what we really are. Psalm 139:1–18 is incredible; it explicitly describes how personal and intimate God knows and loves us as individuals.

> O LORD, you have searched me and you know me. You know when I sit and when I rise; you perceive my thoughts from afar. You discern my going out and my lying down; you are familiar with all my ways. Before a word is on my tongue you know it completely, O LORD. You hem me in—behind and before; you have laid your hand upon me. Such knowledge is too wonderful for me, too lofty for me to attain. Where can I go from your Spirit? Where can I flee from your presence? If I go up to the heavens, you are there; if I make my bed in the depths, you are there. If I rise on the wings of dawn, if I settle on the far side of the sea, even there your hand will guide me, your right hand will hold me fast. If I say, "Surely the darkness will hide me and the light becomes night around me," even the darkness will not be dark to you; the night will shine like the day, for darkness is as light to you. For you created my inmost being; you knit me together in my mother's womb. I praise you because I am fearfully and wonderfully made; your works are wonderful, I know that full well. My frame was not hidden from you when I was made in the secret place. When I was woven

together in the depths of the earth, your eyes saw my unformed body. All the days ordained for me were written in your book before one of them came to be. How precious to me are your thoughts, O God! How vast is the sum of them! Were I count them, they would outnumber the grains of sand. When I awake, I am still with you.

—PSALM 139:1–18

This Psalm has encouraged and strengthened me over the years. If God cared about me and loved me before I was born—while I was in my mother's womb; and if He knows my thoughts and movements before they happen, surely He must be in control of any situation I will ever find myself in. Therefore, I can trust Him with the way things will play out or end.

GOD KNOWS EACH ONE OF US BY NAME

If anybody is really interested in knowing you, one of the first things they want to know is your name. Calling someone by their name ensures you get their attention. There is something about calling people by their name that makes them feel closer to you. That is why people exchange names during introductions, to break that stranger barrier and create some kind of connection. We tend to feel significant, respected, and appreciated if someone remembers our name. By the same token, we tend to be offended with somebody who keeps forgetting, especially over and over again.

Of the vast number of people on earth today, God knows every single one of us fully and completely, just as if there was only just one of us. God knows us collectively, and He also knows us as individuals. God does not care about skin color, race, or ethnicity. As far as He is concerned, there is only one race—the human race. It is made up of many unique and precious individuals that He loves so much that He sent His Son Jesus to die for, so that He could adopt them as His children.

Of God's many perspectives, this is one that if we lived by it, would help us in our relations with one another. It would change the way we view and treat other people. As many as we are, God always has time for each of us on a personal and individual basis. Jesus likens Himself to a good shepherd who calls out to each and every one of His sheep as He takes them where He wants them to go. He says,

> "The watchman opens the gate for him, and the sheep listen to his voice. He calls his own sheep by name and leads them out."
>
> —John 10:3

God Has an Individual Plan for Your Life

God cares about you so much. You are always on His mind. He can't get enough of you. He can never be bored or tired with us. His love for us is everlasting and unconditional. If God cares about birds of the air and lilies of the field, surely you can imagine how much more He cares about and pays attention to every detail of your life. Jesus says in Matthew 10:30, "And even the very hairs of your head are all numbered." That's how intimate and personal God knows and loves you. Just imagine: you wake up in the morning and wash your hair; when you comb it, some of it falls off. God is keeping count! If He pays such detailed attention to your hair, can you picture how much more He cares about the major areas in your life? He knows about your current situation. He knows about your failing health. He knows about your financial situation. He knows about your marriage and your career. Whatever it is, He knows about it and He cares!

If you call upon Him in faith and hang in there, He will deliver you. Meanwhile, always know that He will give you peace and His grace will sustain you. To each one of us, God has a predestined plan for our lives. Whatever He calls us to do, He will enable and empower us to achieve it. That is real success, when you live a life God intended for you to live from the very beginning.

Jeremiah was a prophet chosen by God to warn the Israelites against continuing in sin and worshiping idols. Although he knew God had chosen him, Jeremiah still felt inadequate and unqualified for the task. God reminded him that before he was born, He approved him and specifically anointed him for this. This is what God told him: "Before I formed you in the womb I knew you, before you were born I set you apart; I appointed you as a prophet to the nations" (Jer. 1:5).

God's plan for our lives is always for good, He only wants the best for us. In spite of life's challenges, we are always guaranteed His presence, peace, and joy that keeps us together and strong, whether or not we get the outcome we were hoping for. If we yield to the Holy

Spirit and live by the Word of God, we will be guided to our individual predestined journeys.

God went on to remind the prophet that despite the hardships and challenges he was facing, His plan for him (and us) never changes. He says,

> "For I know the plans I have for you," declares the
> LORD, "plans to prosper you and not to harm you,
> plans to give you hope and a future."
> —JEREMIAH 29:11

Although sometimes in life we may feel more harm than good and the future may appear more bleak than prosperous, that's not God's intended plan for us. He clearly states that He wants to prosper us and to do us no harm. It could be that we are going through life's tribulations and trials, but God is still in control and His plans would not have changed. Praise God for Jesus Christ who overcame, and He is the one who provides us with peace in the presence of life's storms.

> Even though I walk through the valley of the
> shadow of death, I will fear no evil, for you are
> with me; your rod and your staff, they comfort me.
> —PSALM 23:4

God wants us to be more and more like Jesus. Everything that happens in our lives, whether good or bad, can be an opportunity for us to be refined and transformed into His likeness—if we keep our eyes focused on Him. Paul says,

And we know that in all things God works for the good of those who love him, who have been called according to his purpose. For those God foreknew he also predestined to be conformed to the likeness of his Son, that he might be the first born among many brothers.

—ROMANS 8:28–29

No one likes trials; they are not fun. But the reality is that we will encounter them even within our identity as the children of God. How we deal with them is what separates us from the rest of the world. We always have hope that God's plans for our lives are always for good.

Chapter 11

WE ARE CHRIST'S AMBASSADORS

SOMEONE ONCE DEFINED Christianity as knowing Christ and letting Him be known. Jesus came to the earth and died on the cross so that humanity can be saved. You and I are born again today because somebody was faithful enough to share the gospel of Jesus with us. It does not matter how it was channeled—whether through the media, in print, or in person, the most important thing is that we heard the good news through somebody doing exactly what Jesus commanded us believers to do. In Mark 16:15, "He said to them, 'Go into all the world and preach the good news to all creation.'"

As God's beloved children, we have been commanded and given the responsibility of letting Christ be known to others. It is up to us believers to tell a dying world about our Savior, Jesus Christ. God is relying on us to be His mouthpiece to our families, at the workplace, in our communities, and just about wherever people are. We have to use our hearts, our mouths, our resources, and our feet to proclaim the good news.

As believers, we are called to be Christ's ambassadors. An ambassador is an appointed representative of a country in a foreign land. He represents his country's sovereignty and values, and he communicates these to others. We represent, testify, and communicate to the world our Lord and Savior, Jesus Christ, who was crucified so that we can be reconciled to God. The apostle Paul says,

> All this is from God, who reconciled us to himself through Christ, and gave us the ministry of reconciliation: that God was reconciling the world to himself in Christ, not counting men's sins against them. And he has committed to us the message of reconciliation. We are therefore Christ's ambassadors, as though Christ were making his appeal through us. We implore you on Christ's behalf: Be reconciled to God.
>
> —2 CORINTHIANS 5:18–20

There are people who have heard something about Jesus, others believe He was one of the prophets who lived and died a long time ago, and there are some who believe that just because they go to church they are automatically saved. That's where we come in; not to argue and debate about Jesus but to simply testify of our Lord according to the Word of God and then leave the rest to Him. We don't have to coax or force people into salvation. Jesus touches people's hearts all by Himself. This is what He says in John 12:32, "But I, when I am lifted up from the earth, will draw all men to myself." God uses us as channels and vessels for spreading the gospel, but He does the saving himself.

God Wants All Men to Repent

No one knows for sure when Jesus is coming back. The Bible says He will come like a thief, unannounced. But as each day passes and from the signs around us, we know we are drawing nearer to His second coming. As believers we wait in anticipation for that day when we will finally meet with our Lord Jesus face to face; and this is good. But instead of just waiting, how about if we utilize this time to tell as many people as we possibly can about the gospel of Jesus Christ? God sent Him in the flesh to die for all mankind; this includes us, our neighbors, our work colleagues, our friends, our relatives, and the people we meet on the streets. Why not reach out to them so that they too can be saved and experience this amazing love and grace?

Paul says we have to pray and intercede for everybody in this regard. "This is good, and pleases God our Savior, who wants all men to be saved and come to a knowledge of the truth" (1 Tim. 2:3–4). Despite the debate that is sometimes raised that not all men are meant to be saved because only those chosen by God will be saved and respond to the gospel, I think as believers we should just proclaim the gospel of Jesus Christ to everybody and leave the rest to God. I honestly don't believe that He will be disappointed and punish us for sharing the good news with those not "chosen" to be saved, if this makes any sense.

LOVE SHOULD COMPEL US

I love my family so much that the thought of them languishing in hell deeply disturbed me. So I embarked on a mission to tell them about Jesus, and most of them got saved. I am grateful to God for that. Some of them have since passed on, but I am comforted in the knowledge that we will meet in heaven again. For those who have not yet given their lives to Christ, I continue to pray for them. I have not given up on them. I believe I have done my part; a seed has been planted. It is Jesus Himself through the Holy Spirit who convicts men to repent. Our job is to open our mouths to proclaim the good news and to pray for them.

Jesus commanded us to love one another. If we really love people, we will want them to be saved. In John 13:34 He says, "A new commandment I give you: Love one another. As I have loved you, so you must love one another." It is love that drove Jesus to the cross, and it is love that enabled Him to bear the weight of the sin of the world on His shoulders. Through the Holy Spirit, love has been given to us so that we can reach out to others as we do what Jesus commanded us to do. Therefore, we can do it because His love dwells in us richly.

In Romans 5:5 Paul tells us, "God has poured out his love into our hearts by the Holy Spirit, whom he has given us." This makes it possible to love other people even if we were formerly unloving or not a people person. It is this love that motivated Paul to continue preaching the gospel in the face of hardships and persecutions.

> For Christ's love compels us, because we are convinced that one died for all, and therefore all died. And he died for all, and those who live should no longer live for themselves but for him who died for them and was raised again.
>
> —2 CORINTHIANS 5:14–15

God loves people. We may disappoint Him at times, but He continues to love us and yearn for a relationship with us. As His children we inherited this loving nature from Him. Therefore, we too should be driven by this love to reach out to the lost souls. Seriously, God is relying on you and me to do our part. Out there in the world are people living chaotic lifestyles, trying and experimenting with everything and anything, and running and searching hoping to bump into something that will finally bring meaning and sense into their lives. All they are searching for is Christ, really. It can be disguised as searching for power, recognition, or aspiring to reach one's full potential; but only our Lord and Savior Jesus Christ can truly provide us with these things. And above all, only He can bring meaning and purpose to life. Consequently, we should be steering people toward Jesus, for them to experience that fullness and richness in life.

We should be passionate about what our heavenly Father is passionate about—people. God sees all the lost souls and He cares for them deeply. And that is why He empowered us to proclaim the good news to them. Unfortunately, not every believer is taking heed to this call. This is what Jesus says:

> When he saw the crowds, he had compassion on
> them, because they were harassed and helpless,
> like sheep without a shepherd. Then he said to the
> disciples, "The harvest is plentiful but the workers
> are few."
>
> —Matthew 9:36–37

We are the workers, you and I, as believers and children of God. We have to love people enough to act on that love. Not just by word only, but our actions ought to back that love. Every day we encounter people; therefore, there are many opportunities for us to do what God wants us to do. We can't leave this job for the pastors and evangelists only. They are doing their part; we have to do ours. Not every believer is called to have a pulpit ministry, but every believer is called to be a witness for Christ. There are some people that pastors and evangelists cannot reach but whom we can encounter as we go about our daily businesses.

People who are lost may be searching for Christ without knowing it, as they seek the meaning of life and to fill that inner void that nothing but Christ can fill. That's where you and I come in. We have to live our daily lives in a way that reflects a resurrected Savior as we share with them that He is the source of life, peace, joy, and fulfillment.

> How, then, can they call on the one they have not
> believed in? And how can they believe in the one
> of whom they have not heard? And how can they
> hear without someone preaching to them? And
> how can they preach unless they are sent? As it is

written, "How beautiful are the feet of those who
bring good news."

—ROMANS 10:14–15

Therefore we cannot underestimate the importance
of sharing our own experiences with Jesus with others.
Instead of judging them, we have to love them and bring
them to the knowledge of Jesus Christ. It could be just
what they are looking for. Ministering to others should
not be seen as a Christian task or duty, it is part of who
we are and what we do as God's children. We have to be
faithful and obedient enough to do what our Lord commanded us to do before He ascended to heaven. And
the Holy Spirit will help us accomplish that effectively.
Acts 1:8 says, "But you will receive power when the Holy
Spirit comes on you; and you will be my witnesses in
Jerusalem, and in all Judea and Samaria, and to the ends
of the earth."

To every human being who finds Jesus Christ, it is a
big deal in heaven. They go into celebration mode. One
more person rescued from the blazing, unquenchable
fires of hell is no joke. God loves people; hence one soul
added into His kingdom is cause for celebration. Jesus
says,

> "I tell you that in the same way there will be more
> rejoicing in heaven over one sinner who repents
> than over ninety-nine righteous persons who do
> not need to repent."

—LUKE 15:7

The fact that God rejoices over one sinner who repents and enters into a relationship with Him also serves to show how much He values, treasures, and loves us as individuals. We love others because He loved us first and deposited that loving nature inside every one of us. While we are reaching out to others with this love, He will take care of us, restore us, and replenish us.

Chapter 12

WE ARE LIVING EPISTLES
FOR CHRIST

AN EPISTLE IS a letter. Most of the New Testament is made up of epistles written by the apostle Paul to different churches, groups of people, and individuals to convey messages. As believers we are called to be living epistles to the world. Paul reminded the Corinthians that because they had received Jesus Christ, they were now epistles read by everybody.

> You yourselves are our letter, written on our hearts, known and read by everybody. You show that you are a letter from Christ, the result of our ministry, written not with ink but with the Spirit of the living God, not on tablets of stone but on tablets of human hearts.
>
> —2 CORINTHIANS 3:2–3

At salvation the Spirit of God comes to minister life to our human hearts. How we live our lives outwardly depends on what is inside of us. That is why Proverbs 4:23 says, "Above all else, guard your heart, for it is the wellspring of life." Whatever is inside you is bound to come out on the outside. People tell what kind of a person you are by "reading" your actions. That is why we are cautioned to guard our hearts, to be mindful of what we store inside of us, which has the power to influence our behavior. This is what the Bible refers to as "the wellspring of life." To the children of God, the Spirit is our wellspring of life. It is our source of life; therefore, people should be able to see and read that from the way we live our daily lives. We have to make a deliberate choice to cooperate with the Holy Spirit in order to live outwardly what has been deposited in us. It won't happen automatically.

The World Is Watching Us

It is well known that people in the world (and other Christians) are watching the way we live our lives, and it is from this that they draw conclusions about our faith and the God we serve. We can either impress them or repulse them with our actions. If our behaviors, especially from Monday to Saturday, are the complete opposite of the way we behave in church or in front of other brethren, then we risk being labeled as hypocrites. And this does little to motivate anyone to be a believer.

People hate fake Christians. Christianity is a lifestyle, it's our identity. Therefore, there should be nothing fake or phony about it. If we are not led by the Spirit of God, then it means the flesh is the one controlling us with consequent "fruits" and results that are clear to everybody else.

> The acts of the sinful nature are obvious: sexual immorality, impurity and debauchery, idolatry and witchcraft; hatred, discord, jealousy, fits of rage, selfish ambition, dissentions, factions and envy; drunkenness, orgies and the like. I warn you, as I did before, that those who live like this will not inherit the kingdom of God.
>
> —GALATIANS 5:19–21

We have the Spirit of our resurrected Savior. He comes to give us life to the full. He is our source of peace and joy. He gives us a new identity when we receive and believe in Him—we become Christians. Therefore, we have to reflect His nature and characteristics. And this is possible when He is the one leading and guiding us. When we live like this, we bear fruits of the Spirit that are obvious and can be read by everybody.

> But the fruit of the Spirit is love, joy, peace, patience, kindness, goodness, faithfulness, gentleness and self control.
>
> —GALATIANS 5:22–23

When people read these characteristics and behaviors in our lives, they can conclude that indeed we are Christians. These are the characteristics that are synonymous with our Christ. And since His Spirit is in us, when we allow Him to lead us, we will be able to live outwardly His very nature that is within us. In a world where it is dog-eat-dog and an "eye for an eye" attitudes, fruits of the Spirit set us apart. They have the power to attract the lost toward our faith, because they will want what we have.

WE ARE NOT OF THIS WORLD

In the fast paced age we currently live in, if we are not careful, there are many things that can be distractions and can become obstacles in our walk with God. The world is constantly changing. There is always new technology. And people's value systems are evolving such that some things that used to be private or frowned upon are now acceptable to some and even paraded in public.

Some of the changes are actually good and beneficial and help to make our lives much easier and simpler. However, the devil is also taking advantage of the situation by ensuring that people (some believers included) broaden their level of tolerance. We get accustomed to things and behaviors so that we flinch less and less and become not overly shocked by what is really taboo and is an abomination in the sight of God.

On the other hand there are lots of good things happening as well. As Christians, we have to filter what is clean from what is rubbish. It's our responsibility to choose what we want to see, hear, touch, feel, and smell because the devil lures us through all the senses in order to lure us toward darkness. Apart from the fact that indulging the flesh can contradict or grieve the Spirit of God, another problem with the flesh is that it can never be quenched or satisfied long term. The more you give in to it, the more it thirsts and demands from you until it gains control over you. The devil knows this and uses it as bait.

With so much technology around, all anybody needs to do to satisfy curiosity, their dark side, or a perverse need is to sit in front of a computer, phone, or other gadget. Technology in itself is good, it's how and what you use it for that makes the big difference. Technology is helping us to express our faith, to reach out to a broader population; and it's also helping us with our communication systems. It is being our friend that way. But it can also be our foe and cause our downfall when abused or utilized to indulge fleshly and carnal desires.

We should be able to discern right from wrong and truth from deception. We are the children of the light. What happens when you shine light into darkness? It brings clarity and light and has a pulling force toward it. We have been called to draw people to the truth, to this light. If we fail to shine our lights, we risk being the ones being drawn into the darkness. There are lots of temptations in the world and they too have a pulling and luring force. We have seen good Christians backslide as a result. Seeking and running after worldly pleasures and indulging every fleshly desire can draw you away from enjoying an intimate relationship with God. The Bible warns us to be mindful of this.

> Do not love the world or anything in the world.
> If anyone loves the world, the love of the Father
> is not in him. For everything in the world—the
> cravings of sinful man, the lust of his eyes and
> the boasting of what he has and does—comes not

from the Father but from the world. The world and
its desires pass away, but the man who does the
will of the Father lives forever.

—1 John 2:15–17

We have been saved from the pit of hell and darkness. Then why go there to dip your toes once in a while? We have the real deal in us; we should never allow the devil to entice us back into the snare in the name of pleasure and keeping up with the world. That would make us double minded Christians and hypocrites—when we claim to love God with all our hearts but at the same time partake in whatever the world has to offer.

If we claim to have fellowship with him yet walk in
the darkness, we lie and not live by the truth.

—1 John 1:6

In our quest to follow Christ and righteous living, we will ruffle a few feathers because not everyone will be happy with our decision to do so. You can expect this reaction from some family members, spouses, neighbors, work colleagues, and the like. This could be due to a number of reasons, including that they are used to the old us, used to us being part of them and doing certain things together; or they might simply be opposed to our faith altogether. Maybe before they knew how to handle us, understood us, and even had us all figured out.

But now that we are born again and have made a decision to change our lives to align with the Word and will of God, that's when problems may arise. We may cease to do certain things, such as laughing at and making rude jokes, drinking and doing drugs, partying all night, or whatever it is we were into before. Instead, we begin to spend time with God, praying and worshiping. We refine our language and choose different programs to watch. We lose a few friends who might draw us back.

Of course some people will hate you for the new changes you will be making. This happens especially if they do not understand your faith or have misconceptions about it. The apostle Peter addressed this:

> Therefore, since Christ suffered in his body, arm yourselves also with the same attitude, because he who has suffered in his body is done with sin. As a result, he does not live the rest of his earthly life for evil human desires, but rather for the will of God. For you have spent enough time in the past doing what pagans choose to do—living in debauchery, lust, drunkenness, orgies, carousing and detestable idolatry. They think it strange that you do not plunge with them into the same flood of dissipation, and they heap abuse on you.
>
> —1 PETER 4:1–4

But you should not let their actions discourage you; their behavior is a sign that you have consecrated yourself for God and have removed yourself from the world and its passions. So what if the world hates you for loving God and choosing a lifestyle that glorifies Him? Jesus says the world hated Him too for that.

> If the world hates you, keep in mind that it hated
> me first. If you belonged to the world, it would love
> you as its own. As it is, you do not belong to the
> world, but I have chosen you out of the world. That
> is why the world hates you.
>
> —John 15:18–19

It is important to keep in mind that though the world may hate us because of our life changing decision, we, however, as the children of God are called to reach out in love to them instead of hating them back. We have to pray for them. And, hopefully, they too will be drawn toward the kingdom as they see the positive changes in our lives. That is what God wants us to do as ambassadors and living epistles.

Chapter 13

WE ARE CALLED TO IMITATE CHRIST

WE HAVE ESTABLISHED that we are called to be Christ's ambassadors and to be living epistles to the world through the way we live our daily lives. The best way to be His ambassadors and living epistles is through imitating Christ Himself. Not by imitating the pastor, the pastor's wife, the pastor's children, or any other spiritual person. Although they may be God-loving, principled, and respected folks, they too ultimately need Jesus as their solid rock and foundation in life and are subject to the same trials and temptations as everybody else. Therefore, it is much safer to choose to imitate Christ from the beginning. There are some Christians who were discouraged in their faith when the person they looked up to did something that disappointed them. They can be role models, but our foundation should be rooted in Christ at all times.

> Be imitators of God, therefore, as dearly loved children and live a life of love, just as Christ loved us

and gave himself up for us as a fragrant offering and sacrifice to God.

—EPHESIANS 5:1–2

Note that the Bible calls us "dearly loved" and instructs us to live by love. Christ loved us first, therefore we can imitate Him and love others as well. Because God is love, we too as Christians should love also. We can't be God's children and yet fail to love.

IT IS POSSIBLE TO LOVE EVERYBODY

In a world full of hatred and malice, love should identify and distinguish us from the rest. Our Lord and Savior, Jesus Christ, walked in love on earth. He associated and dined with the rich, the poor, and sinners. He embraced the noble and the lame alike; He simply loved everybody. Love has many fruits; out of it comes compassion, kindness, mercy, and giving. If we are going to be successful in imitating Christ, we have to start by walking in love first. We love Him because He loved us first. He gave us the Holy Spirit who enables us to love everybody else regardless of who they are and what they are like. Jesus summed it up in two commandments.

> Jesus replied: "'Love the Lord your God with all your heart and with all your soul and with all your mind.' This is the first and greatest commandment. And the second is like it: 'Love your neighbor as yourself.'"
>
> —MATTHEW 22:37–39

When we love people with the love of God, we do so because they are His creations not necessarily because we like them as individuals. For Christians, loving others is a commandment and not an option. Therefore, we need the help of the Holy Spirit to enable us to love even the most unlovable and hostile persons. Love rises above these traits and should move us into praying for the individuals concerned. Jesus loved and prayed for the people who persecuted Him, so He is not asking us to do something that He didn't have to do. He says,

> "But I tell you: Love your enemies and pray for those who persecute you, that you may be sons of your Father in heaven. He causes his sun to rise on the evil and the good, and sends rain on the righteous and the unrighteous."
>
> —MATTHEW 5:44

LOVE FORGIVES

Christians who walk in love are in a better position to achieve so much more for Christ; they bear good fruit, are much happier and peaceful, and they forgive easily. Love enables us to live strife-free lives because we can overlook some minor irritations and not let them steal our peace and joy.

Peter tells us, "Above all, love each other deeply, because love covers a multitude of sins" (1 Peter 4:8). The covering of sins refers to forgiveness and choosing not to be offended, even though we may feel we have every reason to be. Jesus set an example for us by forgiving those who hung Him on the cross. They had shamed, humiliated, and crucified Him beside criminals, but He prayed for them: "Father, forgive them, for they do not know what they are doing" (Luke 23:34).

Joseph chose to forgive his brothers who had mistreated him and sold him into slavery. Instead he loved them and took care of them in the time of famine. When Stephen was stoned for standing up for the truth and proclaiming Jesus Christ as the Savior, he chose to forgive his persecutors at the time of his death and he prayed for them.

> While they were stoning him, Stephen prayed, "Lord Jesus, receive my spirit." Then he fell on his knees and cried out, "Lord, do not hold this sin against them." When he had said this, he fell asleep.
> —ACTS 7:59

As believers and God's children, we can never fully live in peace and freedom if we harbor bitterness, unforgiveness, and quests for revenge to those who mistreat us. This is not easy, but it is possible with prayer and the Holy Spirit who is there to assist us in imitating Christ. God is calling us to a higher level of Christian living and maturity. He wants us to be more and more like His Son. This involves not giving in to the flesh and our feelings and emotions. Paul encourages us "to be made new in the attitude of your minds; and to put on the new self, created to be like God in true righteousness and holiness" (Eph. 4:23–24). In verses 31–32 he continues:

Get rid of all bitterness, rage and anger, brawling and slander, along with every form of malice. Be kind and compassionate to one another, forgiving each other just as in Christ God forgave you.

—EPHESIANS 4:31–32

Chapter 14

THE LORD WILL FIGHT
OUR BATTLES

OUR FATHER CARES about everything that is happening in our lives. Sometimes it may seem like He is far away; but the truth is He is forever present, watching over us. And whenever we call upon Him in times of need, He answers. He knows the road may be rough and bumpy at times, but through His grace, He has already made provisions for His children to rise above and not be weighed down by life's challenges. With every challenge we face, He will provide a way out if we trust Him to take care of it.

In 1 Peter 5:7 the Bible says, "Cast all your anxiety on him because he cares for you." God doesn't want us to be troubled. If we call upon Him and have faith that He will deliver us, we will remain peaceful despite experiencing tough circumstances. This is sensible and beneficial for us because we do not always know when we will get a breakthrough; therefore, it is good for our well-being to remain peaceful and untroubled while waiting on and trusting Him. We are victors and not victims and conquerors and unconquered, all because of Him who died for us and now calls us His own.

When going through difficult times, it is tempting to try to figure things out with our own wisdom and strength and come up with solutions; but God wants us to rely on Him at all times. He knows exactly what will be happening and He knows why some things happen to us. Therefore He is the one with the appropriate solutions to our problems. In our quest to make things right, sometimes we end up making them worse because we may not totally comprehend what is really happening.

We Must Seek Peace Always

God has so many blessings in store for us! However, it is difficult for us to receive, appreciate, and enjoy them if we live in strife. There are some blessings that will never be loosed in our lives until we learn to be peaceful and stay away from strife and bitterness.

It is much easier to be peaceful when everything is going well around us, when no one is mistreating or persecuting us. Conversely, it is a big challenge to remain peaceful in the face of trouble and opposition, abuse, conflict, and ill-treatment. But in all these difficult times, God wants us "seek" peace, which means we are to actively look for means for making peace and maintaining it. Jesus said in Matthew 5:9, "Blessed are the peacemakers, for they will be called sons of God."

Where human relationships are concerned, when conflict arises and we feel taken advantage of, it is easier to find ourselves deep in strife and seeking ways of getting control of the whole situation. Psalm 34:14 encourages us to "turn from evil and do good; seek peace and pursue it." We are not called fight our own battles; instead we ought to be constantly seeking ways to be a blessing to others, to be the salt and light of the world. We are only on this earth for but a season; therefore, we cannot waste valuable time evening up and squaring up with people. We leave that to God; whoever mistreats us will have to answer to Him.

We Do Not Avenge and Fight for Ourselves; God Does

When we have been unfairly treated and had injustice done to us, we should always rest assured that our God will fight on our behalf. When we look at whatever is tormenting us and causing us grief and suffering, we tend to feel dwarfed, powerless, and anticipate gloom.

When the Israelites where standing between the raging Red Sea and the mighty Egyptian army, they were terrified and felt discouraged, powerless, and defeated. They couldn't see a possible way out of their predicament. But their leader Moses encouraged them to trust God to provide a way of delivering them.

> Moses answered the people, "Do not be afraid. Stand firm and you will see the deliverance the Lord will bring you today. The Egyptians you see today you will never see again. The Lord will fight for you; you need only to be still."
>
> —Exodus 14:13–14

And God did deliver them; He parted the Red Sea so that the Israelites could pass through. But when the

Egyptian army hot in pursuit tried to do the same, the wall of water leveled out and they all drowned and died in the sea. God knows when injustice has been done, and He knows when and how to fight for us. Sometimes we may feel like we have been unfairly treated and so we go on to avenge ourselves only to discover that no harm or ill was meant or done to us after all. Then we end up being the ones with blood on our hands. That is why it is always best to leave the fighting and avenging to God. On the other hand, we may think everything is well, when in reality people we trust are doing us harm. God fights for us in this situation too.

Most of the time there is no real satisfaction from revenge; more often than not we are left with feelings of guilt and self-loathing. It's like playing right into the devil's trap and can leave us with more problems to deal with than when we began. Paul tells us:

> Do not take revenge, my friends, but leave room for God's wrath, for it is written: "It is mine to avenge; I will repay," says the Lord.
>
> —Romans 12:19

Our God is above every evil plot the enemy can ever scheme against us. He is mighty and great, and everything is under His control. The forces of darkness have no authority or power over us because of the powerful and precious blood of Jesus. The devil may make his schemes against us, but he can't succeed in destroying us. The blood of Jesus is against him, and his plans will come tumbling down when we call upon the name of Jesus. God says,

> No weapon forged against you will prevail, and you will refute every tongue that accuses you. This is the heritage of the servants of the LORD, and this is their vindication from me, declares the LORD.
>
> —ISAIAH 54:17

ABOUT THE AUTHOR

JULIE NGWABI WAS born in Zimbabwe, Africa. She is the firstborn in a family of five children and grew up in poverty when her father died when she was eleven years old. She assumed responsibility at an early age looking after her siblings while her mother worked hard trying to provide for them. At one stage they faced homelessness. In 1993 she received Christ as Lord and Savior and pursued a deeper relationship and knowledge of God. In 2007 during a prayer service, the Lord laid it onto her heart to write this book. Claim your identity today!

CONTACT THE AUTHOR

E-mail:

juliengwabi@yahoo.com.au

Website:

www.christianidentity.com.au